The Summer Break

Swati Srivastava

Presentation by *BookLeaf Publishing*

Web: www.bookleafpub.com

E-mail: info@bookleafpub.com

ISBN:9789360944827

First edition 2024

DEDICATION

To my Family, my Friends and my Divine.

Forever Grateful,

Swati Srivastava

ACKNOWLEDGEMENT

I owe my gratitude to the luckiest year, the publishers, and the readers. In reality, I would give the credit to my daughter who started school this year. Now you know the secret of how I could get myself at writing and reaching out to you. May these lines find a home within your soul because it's never too late to take a break.

With love
Swati Srivastava

PREFACE

Dear Reader,

At times, we want to say much more than what we say in actuality. As I pen down these poems, I am all the words that you wish to say, see, hear, and feel. Let me remind you of your journey, by just slowing you down this very moment while you read bit by bit, piece by piece. There are vivid themes and stories with a personal touch for you to imagine and relate.

This anthology of poems is all you need to recognize, reflect, and catalyze your emotions. The language used is English, maybe because I never wrote in any other language.

I want this book to reach out to everyone, in multiple languages, to the corners where even the person who doesn't know how to read, would listen through the spoken words of poetry. Each poem is an effort to loosen your shell.

Yours Truly,
Swati Srivastava

Table of Contents

Yellow and Orange

Did you ever see,
the huge summer sun,
spilling all the light,
and blinding your sight.

In seconds of sweep,
It peeks and seeks,
Making us all believe,
How it won't ever leave.

After all the heat,
The longest days,
And Lazy Afternoons,
It brings back the moon.

To them,
It's a star Or a gas-ball,
Sunrise - a fusion,
And Sunset a Delusion?

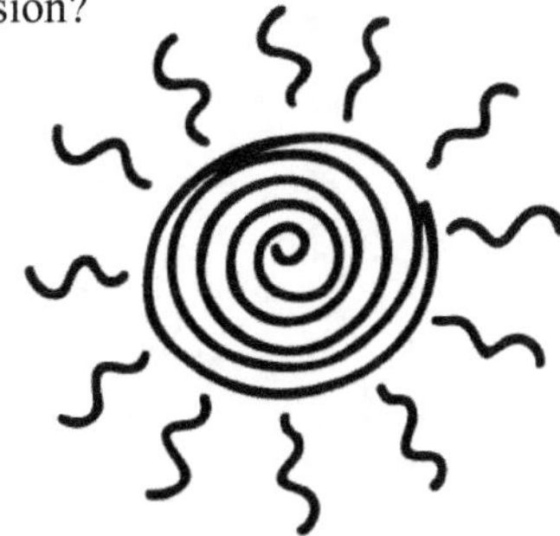

When I was a Kid

Green were the days,
When I was a little kid.
How I spent my time
Picking the limes.

Less expensive were the days,
When I was a little kid.
How I drank fresh juices and shakes,
With not a single waste.

Slow were the days,
When I was a little kid.
How I climbed the trees,
Swinging better than monkeys.

Cool were the days,
When I was a little kid.
How I went to picnic,
Picking dry grasses and sticks.

Seven

5

To me, an ordinary day
the same old hustle
with all the knowns
trying to hide
some secret
behind the cones

Hot and Humid
As it is
with no hint
of slightest wind
up and above
on the highest tips

An over-thinker
Or may be a day-dreamer
got lost in its thoughts
with unheard murmur
Not an ordinary day
I lost her in summer.

Anonymous

call my love
not with the name.
like a warm summer morning
when he looks at me
oh ! how my heart melts !
when he whispers,
words of love
his sparkling eyes
talks to mine.

our hands touch
like a stuck cassette
never wanting to wind.
oh ! how my heart melts !
losing count of years
when did i meet him.

every time when i feel
his heart beat,
i wish he stays
just a little longer
to dance with me.
oh ! how my heart melts !
when he plants
the forehead-kiss,
showering platonic love
on all of me.

how he makes silly names
no wonder he is a star
blinding me all through.
how he places me in
middle of flowery belts
for he already knows
how my heart melts !

Begin

a little girl
who loved to run,
with speed unmatched
while all her peers
watched holding
their breaths.
with all her might,
she could run miles
and break records,
winning all her wins
all at once.
one bad day
when she fell,
and lay flat on road
poor was her strength
weak were her legs
she heard them say.
cuts and bruises
sweat and blood
are part of day,
reaching the cross-line
was all she knew.
things that matter
were the words
not from them
but her own mouth.

how she carried
self with pride,
while all eyes
drooped and stooped
mortified were they.

Why

years after years.
it's not enough,
watching the strips of sky,
I wonder why?

clouds form and deform.
to keep a vow,
which was sworn,
long before the years.

moon wears jewels.
sun wears daisies,
under the same,
star-studded skies.

But, when i see you.
it's not enough,
years after years.
I wonder why?

Footprints

Is it a Déjà vu;
or effect of my brew?
from crawling on fours,
on the tiled floor;
to her treading softly;
was I asleep lately ?

This ain't utopia.
for I have Myopia;
sweetie, you are so close,
little feet on my toes;
tiny hands wrap my fingers,
gentle yet firm like wringer.

I was drowsily mistaken,
steps not yet taken;
waiting for first step of hers,
coffee and marshmallows,
and some irregular stirs !

Wanderer

i still walk through
the busiest streets,
with my violin and bow;
to play the tunes of love,
just nice and slow.

the tensioned strings
release their pain,
as it rests below my chin;
humming the stories
of seasons, and lost grin.

flowing music
guides my way,
as i tap my foot
against the road;
walking amidst of all,
with no fixed abode.

Secrets

speak of a secret
which i don't know.
the one which
you hid at the end
of rainbow.

he spoke
of sun and rays
of days and skies
even the stars too.
but no i love you' s.

the secret of yours,
i was fully aware.
love until-
we're dust and deep;
I'll be the earth,
and the skies you keep.

Shadow

see the star at night
twinkling alone
giving light
surrounding enlightens
while darkness shuns
seems too simple a task
but have you ever asked ?

deep down its core
it burns with sore
keeping the truth within
giving an illusion
from a distance
before you could even sense.

simmering itself
becoming a thing of beauty
silently, it does its duty.
do you wonder
about these mystical stars
or enjoy the picturesque
of the body which mars.

Winged

25

small yet agile
flying here and there,

on the flowers,
on the grass it went,

all through the vast meadows,
crossed a brook,

right in the mid of the opening,
of hundredth anniversary bridge,

hugging spring in all its might,
oh ! i can't see it now.

I fell in love with you,
Ah ! you're out of my sight.

Vacations

when schools were shut,
we got out of rut;
metal onto metal clanked,
while the surroundings danked !

as a finger led me to the house,
all my senses were aroused;
just to meet my gran,
crossing crossings, I ran !

a place to explore,
memories to be adored;
witnessing robbery of hung cloth,
while inhaling the fresh broth !

evening spree to bazaar,
buying candies from filled jars;
tuesdays reserved for Hanuman,
smooth execution of preplans !

Omen

I still remember
the early springs,
how he made me cling,
onto my favorite swings;

with all the power, he bent;
higher and higher, i went;
kissing the sky,
wish i could fly.

that evening was
the final meeting.
he bought me
some glooming daffodils
which he grew himself
below his window-sill.

there was this circling crow
with a sudden snow.
wrong eyes twitched
while he kissed,
leaving me with
an open-stitch.

Ship

when i see you,
i see a poised man;
when i hear you,
i hear a humble man;

I never spake,
of my love; to you.
yet i know,
how you read it all.

you are the calmness
of the deepest ocean.
did you swallow;
some magical potion ?

i chose you,
and you chose me.
together we shall
begin our long journey.

be the anchor
and be the mast;
that's how our
sail would last.

Choices

Is it all about-
the choices we make ?
A head-start
or late-sleeper;
afloat on waters
or diving deeper;
raising a toast
or being a loner;
being in the centre
or at one of the corners ?

boring days turning special
are the lightings going dull ?
favorite food
and a burnt smell,
silent mouth
or a big yell ?

less of me
or less of you;
picking a dress,
pink or blue;
taking a lift,
or a staircase;
it's all about-
the choices we make.

Bloom

One fine day
she raised her brows
asking about the
flowers,
how do they grow ?

in the simplest words
i let her believe
in the birth and death
having finite number
of breaths.

look at the,
push or pulls
of bees and butterflies
how flowers are born
without any cries.

just like babies,
wind makes them
sway and sleep,
while sun makes them
happy and bright.

they craft and hold
the sweetest nectar,
need water and soil
to keep their heads
upright.

one little seed
at a time,
will sprout into
the prettiest flower
in the town !

Tick-Tock

look how far you
have come,
the greatest person,
you could ever become.

dine in the finest
restaurants,
served by your personal
chefs.
best attire adorn
your body,
meanwhile
how your eyes
stare you back
as you sip the
same old coffee.

how your face
lit up at the sight
of me,
brighter than the candle
at the same table,
making you go wobbly
in your knees.

how you told me
lessons,
on how simple a
love could ever be,
money can't buy
happiness
nothing comes back,
not even the daylight
in the far-flung seas.

your four chambers,
look empty
while you wait for me.
i am not coming back,
to that ugly prison,
keep those keys,
while I remain free.

Paws

you know
you read it all,
from the title.
how i will write
about the paws.

but why write of loss,
when you had
the best times
of your lives,
holding those paws.

how those little fours,
would run
door-to-door
in hope of finding
you and the fragrance.

see how cruel
the cycle could ever be,
now you are not here,
to smell the clothes,
i wear.

your favorite
food plate,
lies at the same place,
my eyes are
hallucinating,
all that was served,
you ate.

you are still here,
as your calls
i happily answer.
those tail-wags and kisses
i miss.
I'll let the world know
you were one of the threes
who had cancer.

Date-Night

he is all
in suit and tie,
demarcating -
truth and lie;
here, i stand and stare,
with all my
snarled up hair.

his fragrance cast
a spell,
making me uneasy,
before i fell.
he is approaching,
with resolute steps,
i am all blank,
with no prep.

he bought me the
finest flowers,
and asked my hand,
don't want to leave,
from this fairy-land.

he held my waist,
and pulled me closer
my eyes drowned in his,
while my hand rested
on his crisp blazer.

lights grew fainter,
and music was unheard,
oh ! how i was flying,
like a free bird.
that whole night,
i couldn't sleep;
how you swept me,
off my feet !

Blackhole

each passing day; a memory
doesn't matter; good or bad
today, you walk in chivalry
like a bishop;
auratic and well-clad.

an year of mixed events
with smooth and sharp bents
let us not look back
into the dead sack.

"let the dead past bury its dead"
this line, I swallow
of the bard, Mister Longfellow
for, it was clearly said.

if you try and mess,
you shall lose and digress
with your stumbling soul
rolling and falling
into the blackhole.

Next

bundles of words,
just like logs of wood;
i carry the heavy load,
on the unnamed road.

what would i write next,
to some it is mere text,
let me shed some light;
i was born to write.

how i tell your stories
as mine,
all our lives
are the parallel lines.

may your day
be as bright
as your face,
may you read
each day,
and slow down
from the race.

think about the lines,
quit all the whines,
time for business;
time for money.
But, no time
for yourself honey !

www.ingramcontent.com/pod-product-compliance
Lightning Source LLC
La Vergne TN
LVHW021239200726
843509LV00012B/1534